Marvellous Maths
Subtraction

By Alison Wells

Illustrations by Richard Maccabe

CHERRYTREE BOOKS

A Cherrytree Book

Adapted by A S Publishing from
Discovering Math
First published by Benchmark Books
Copyright © Marshall Cavendish Corporation 1996
Series created by Blackbirch Graphics Inc
Series editor: Tanya Lee Stone

This edition first published in 1997
by Cherrytree Press Ltd
a subsidiary of
The Chivers Company Ltd
Windsor Bridge Road
Bath BA2 3AX

British Library Cataloguing in Publication Data
Wells, Alison
    Subtraction
    1. Subtraction—Juvenile literature 2. Subtraction—Problems,
exercises, etc.—Juvenile literature
    I. Title
    372.7'2

ISBN 0 7451 5315 1

Printed and bound in the USA

Contents

Paper Pitch

Here's a great trick to play. First, tell your family that you have amazing powers. Explain that you will be able to tell how many paper pellets are in a bag – *without looking inside.* They will probably want you to prove it. Here's how:

• Make some small paper pellets from waste paper.

• Stand a bin or bag against a wall.

• Stand five giant steps away from the bag.

• Take fifteen paper pellets and toss them, one at a time, into a bag.

• Count the number of pieces that miss the bag. Take away the number that missed from the fifteen you started with. The remainder are in the bag.

• Make your prediction to your family. Then get someone to look in the bag to see if you were right. Ta da!

• Prove that you can do this amazing trick again and again. Each time, you will be able to predict correctly the number of paper pellets that are in the bag.

If someone says, 'That's truly amazing', you can say, 'No. That's subtraction'.

Card Smart

You really will have to be 'card smart' to figure out these card puzzles. Get a pack of cards and deal out these hands.

• Add up the numbers shown on the cards in each hand.

• Take away one card from each hand (and subtract its value) so that the sum of the two remaining cards for all four hands is the same number. What's the number?

Now try this set of hands.

• What's the magic number?

• Can you make up your own hand of spades to fit the puzzle?

Draughts Duel

Have you ever played draughts? Even if you haven't, here's a draughts duel to test your wits.

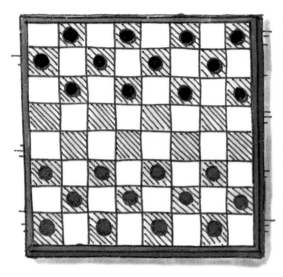

Here are some tips before you start. There are two players – Black and Red. Each tries to take the other player's draughts. The player who manages to take all the other player's pieces wins the game. At the beginning of a game, the board looks like this. Make your own board if you haven't got one.

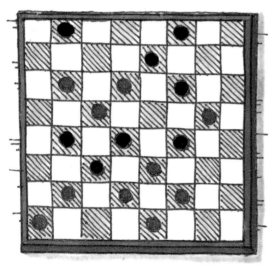

Now let's imagine a game has begun. Use bottle caps and coins to act out the game, if you have no draughts. You will need twelve of each. Players stick to the black squares and take turns to move. They can move diagonally only.

Who is ahead? How far ahead? How do you know?

The game continues. Each player has now taken several more pieces. Here are the pieces that have been taken:

- How many draughts does Red have left on the board?

- How many draughts does Black have left on the board?

- How many more draughts does Red have left on the board than Black?

- How many more draughts does Black have to take in order to have taken the same number as Red?

The Gremlin's Gold

Here's a game for two to four players. You will need to make two spinners like these. Push a short pencil or cocktail stick through the centre.

Here's how the game goes. A gremlin found fifty pieces of gold. He hurried to hide them in his cave, but he dropped some along the way.

Your goal is to get as many gold pieces as you can. You can get gold by being first to land on squares with gold or by getting to the cave first. Each player will need a marker to move. Put pennies or bits of paper on the squares and in the cave to represent the gold.

This is where it gets tricky! This could be 18-9 or 10-9 or 18-2 or 10-2.

• Spin to see who goes first. The player with the highest spin on the higher numbers spinner goes first.

• Spin both spinners. Subtract one of the numbers on the smaller numbers spinner from one of the numbers on the larger numbers spinner. This tells you how many squares to move. Each time you spin, there are four possible moves. Pick the one that helps you land on gold, or avoid losing gold.

• If you are the first to land on a square with gold, you take the gold. If you land on a 'lose gold' square, you must give up the amount of gold (if you have it) and put it on the square. The next player to land there can take it. To get the gold in the gremlin's cave, your move must be exact, not over. Good luck!

8

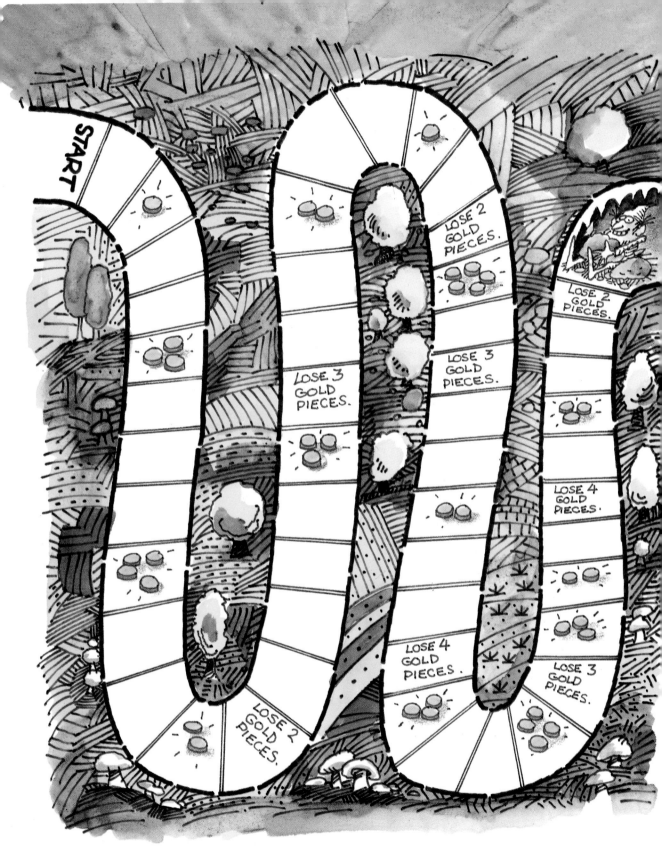

It's Nothing, Really!

Take any four numbers. For example, try these:

Subtract each number from the one next to it. Then subtract the numbers at the beginning and end of the row.

Hint: Always subtract the smaller number from the larger number.

It's nothing. Really!

Write your answers in a row below the numbers you started with, like this:

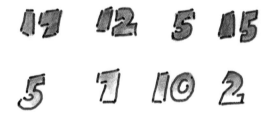

Keep subtracting in the same way until you can go no further.

• How many rows do you end up with?

• What happened in the last two rows?

Try this trick with four different numbers. Does it work? Do it again and amaze your friends.

Pasta Puzzle

How well do you know your pasta? People in Italy have been eating pasta for more than 700 years? It comes in all different shapes and sizes.

Spaghetti is long and thin. Lasagna is wide and flat.

You could use real spaghetti and lasagna for this, but it is probably easier to cut paper strips instead.

One piece of lasagna stands for a ten and one piece of spaghetti stands for a one. Can you tell what numbers these pasta shapes stand for?

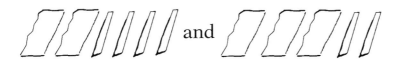

Now try to solve these pasta problems.

• Draw a picture of your answers.

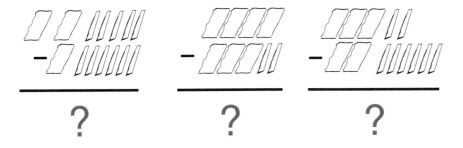

The Tortoise, the Hare and...

In the story of the tortoise and the hare, the moral was 'slow but steady wins the race'. But have you ever wondered who's really faster than whom in the animal kingdom? Some animals might surprise you!

• Use the clues to figure out the speed of each of the animals in miles per hour.

• Rank the animals from 1 to 10 (fastest to slowest).

• Stump your friends. See if they can put the animals in the right order.

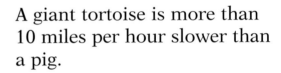

A giant tortoise is more than 10 miles per hour slower than a pig.

A rabbit's pace is 35 miles per hour slower than a cheetah's.

A pig is 2 miles per hour faster than a chicken.

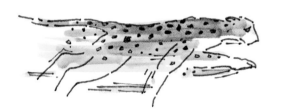

The cheetah is the fastest land animal. It can run at speeds of 70 miles per hour.

A lion can run 15 miles per hour faster than a rabbit.

A cat is 20 miles per hour slower than a lion.

A chicken is 21 miles per hour slower than a cat.

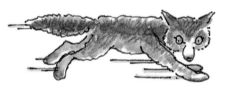

A fox runs 7 miles per hour slower than a lion.

A giraffe is 11 miles per hour slower than a fox.

A human runs between 7 and 8 miles per hour slower than a rabbit.

Tally charts make it easy to keep track of things. Each / is one. Each /// is five.

Red Alert

What's your favourite colour? How popular do you think it is? Here's a way to find out.

Let's say your favourite colour is red. You could take a survey to see how many people are wearing red. If you made a chart of your results, here's what it might look like:

Red	No Red
//// //// //// ||	//// //// //// //// //// //// ///

• How many people wore red? How many did not? Which group was larger? How much larger?

Are you ready to do a survey of your own? Choose any colour you like. Make a chart like the one on page 14. Now all you need is a place where you can watch and tally. A library, park or sports centre might work well. Try to count at least fifty people.

• How many people did you count? How many wore your favourite colour? How many did not? Which group was larger? How much larger?

If you like, tally with a friend whose favourite colour is different from yours. Make sure you record the same people.

• Compare your results. How many wore your favourite colour? How many wore your friend's favourite? How many wore neither? Which group was larger? How much larger?

Tower Challenge

How high is 150 centimetres? Let's
see if you can build a tower that tall
that doesn't topple. You will need
a friend, some 'building blocks'
and a measuring tape at least
1.5 metres long.

The idea is for each of you to try to build a tower exactly 1.5 metres tall.

• Collect objects, such as boxes and books, that you think, when stacked, will measure about 1.5 metres.

• Stack your objects. If your tower keeps toppling, try putting it in a corner.

• Measure each stack. How much over or under 1.5 metres is each stack? Whose stack is closer to 1.5 metres? How much closer?

• Try to get closer to 1.5 metres by replacing one of your objects with a different one.

• Measure again. Now how much over or under is each stack? Whose stack is closer to 1.5 metres? How much closer?

• Keep going. Replace one item at a time and re-measure until someone gets to 1.5 metres exactly.

Shopping Spree

Congratulations! You have just won a £150 shopping spree at a local department store. There are a few rules that you must follow in order to win:

• You may choose only one item in each department.

• You must choose items that, when subtracted from £150, will leave you with £0. No more, and no less.

Get ready to sprint – mathematically. On your mark, get set, GO!

• There are seven different ways to get from £150 to £0 exactly. How many can you find?

19

Pocket Money

Look in your pocket. Find any loose change?
Four children – James, Kelly, Rachel and
Imran – each found five coins in their pockets.
It's up to you to figure out which coins belong
to which child.

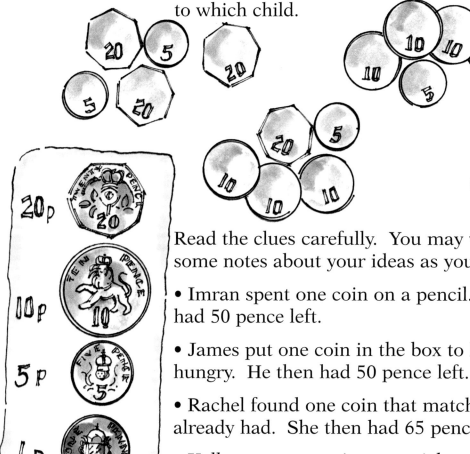

Whose head is on
the other side of
these coins?

Read the clues carefully. You may want to take
some notes about your ideas as you go along.

• Imran spent one coin on a pencil. He then
had 50 pence left.

• James put one coin in the box to help the
hungry. He then had 50 pence left.

• Rachel found one coin that matched three she
already had. She then had 65 pence.

• Kelly spent one coin on a sticker. She then had
four coins that were alike.

• James and Imran have exactly the same coins
now. But if Imran finds 20p, he'll be back where
he started.

Whose coins are whose?

Gallons of Guppies

Once upon a time there were two guppies, George and Hazel, who lived quite happily in a small fish bowl. Before long, they had babies, and their babies had babies. George and Hazel were a little crowded.

This is where YOU enter the picture. Let's suppose there are 500 guppies in all. It is your job to give them away. You'll give away one guppy on the first day, two guppies on the second day, three guppies on the third day, and so on.

• How many days will it take you to give away all the guppies?

• Will you be able to complete the pattern with your last giveaway? (In other words, by following the pattern exactly can you get to 0?)

• Try a different giveaway pattern of your own. Describe it. How many days will it take to give away all the guppies? Does following your pattern exactly get you to 0?

And the Answer is...

Here are some tricks that are bound to make your friends and family stop and wonder if you have magical powers. So drum up an audience, and let the show begin!

• Write the numbers 198 and 3087 on separate pieces of paper and fold them. Give them to different people to hold. (No peeking.) Now, here's the hard part. Remember who has which number!

$$876$$
$$-\ 678$$
$$\overline{198}$$

• Ask someone to give you any three-digit number, such as 543 or 876, in which the digits are consecutive from high to low.

• Get them to watch as you reverse the number (so that it reads from low to high) and subtract it from the number they gave you. You may want to use a calculator.

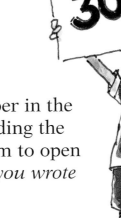

• Ask your audience to read the number in the display. Then point to the person holding the paper with 198 written on it. Get them to open the paper and read the answer – *that you wrote down before you even started.*

Now your audience is warmed up. Time for trick number two.

• Ask someone to give you a four-digit number in which the digits are consecutive from high to low.

• Get the crowd to watch as you reverse the digits and subtract that number from the first number.

$$
\begin{array}{r}
5432 \\
- \ 2345 \\
\hline
3087
\end{array}
$$

• Once again, show the display. Ask the person with the remaining piece of paper to open it and read the answer.

Take a big bow to the thunderous applause of your audience.

Code Breaking

People have been using codes to send secret messages for almost as long as there has been written language. The Arabs developed a code system more than 1,200 years ago. In Europe, codes first became popular about 600 years ago. They were used by governments to send secret instructions and reports to their representatives in other countries.

And as long as there have been codes, there have been code breakers. Here is your chance to break a code. You will need a calculator.

To read a word, turn your calculator upside down.

• Look at the secret message on the next page. See how many words are missing? Your job is to figure out those words.

• Each missing word is represented by a subtraction problem. Enter the problem on your calculator. The answer that is displayed will spell out the missing word.

• On a separate piece of paper, write down each word as you discover it.

• When you have figured out all the words, you are ready to break the code. What does the message say?

$$\begin{array}{r} 8964 \\ -1246 \\ \hline \end{array}$$

Dear

$$\begin{array}{r} 5926 \\ -2419 \\ \hline \end{array}$$

Quick! There is no time to

$$\begin{array}{r} 46785 \\ -11778 \\ \hline \end{array}$$
$$\begin{array}{r} 721 \\ -114 \\ \hline \end{array}$$

Put the map under

$$\begin{array}{r} 8231 \\ -517 \\ \hline \end{array}$$
$$\begin{array}{r} 7491 \\ -2185 \\ \hline \end{array}$$

on the   . If all   well.

$$\begin{array}{r} 543296 \\ -225759 \\ \hline \end{array}$$
$$\begin{array}{r} 9538 \\ -1803 \\ \hline \end{array}$$

will pick it up and   it

$$\begin{array}{r} 348 \\ -347 \\ \hline \end{array}$$
$$\begin{array}{r} 1136 \\ -498 \\ \hline \end{array}$$

you to follow this plan,

$$\begin{array}{r} 4762 \\ -1189 \\ \hline \end{array}$$

or   !   Good luck.

$$\begin{array}{r} 1204 \\ -396 \\ \hline \end{array}$$

A-Maze-ing 10,000

Here's a maze to tax your brain cells. Don't use a calculator!

• Put a piece of thin paper over the maze so that you can read the numbers and see the lines through it.

• Begin at 10,000. Try to find a path that will get you to zero exactly.

• Trace your path. Do all the subtraction in your head as you go along. You may not retrace your path along a line. And remember, if at first you don't succeed.... You know. There may be more than one correct path.

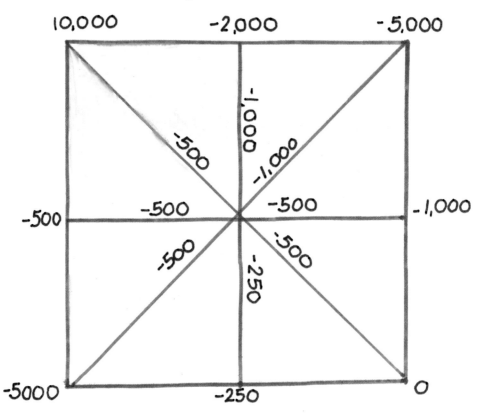

Answers

Page 4 Paper Pitch

If you are getting all of the pellets into the bag every time, you're standing too close. If you aren't getting any in, you're standing too far away. If one of your predictions is wrong, check between the bag and the wall; maybe a pellet got stuck. If your prediction is still wrong, line up fifteen pellets and then take away the number that missed the bag. What's left should be the number you found in the bag.

5 Card Smart

In the first set of hands, the hearts' sum is 15; take away the 8 and you have a remainder of 7. The diamonds' sum is 17; take away the 10 and you have a remainder of 7. The clubs' sum is 12; take away the 5 and you have a remainder of 7. The spades' sum is 14; take away the 7 and you have a remainder of 7.

In the second set of hands, the hearts' sum is 18; take away the 9 and you have a remainder of 9. The diamonds' sum is 12; take away the 3 and you have a remainder of 9. The clubs' sum is 14; take away the 5 and you have a remainder of 9.

Did you come up with a spades hand? Here's one possibility. There are many others.

6/7 Draughts Duel

Red is ahead. Red has 10 pieces left on the board and Black has 8; Red is 2 ahead of Black. You could find this out by covering up a Black and Red piece until you run out of Black pieces; the board would then show how many more Red pieces there are than Black: 2.

Answers

Whenever you find 'how many are left' you use subtraction. In this case, you start with 12 draughts (the number each player had at the beginning of the game) and take away the number of Red draughts in the pile (5). This leaves 7 draughts on the board.

In the same way, you can find that Black has only 5 draughts left on the board (12 take away 7).

You can write equations to show what we have done:

12	and	12
-5		-7
7		5

Whenever you compare two numbers, as you do when you find 'how many more' you use subtraction, too. To find how many more draughts Red has than Black, you subtract the number of draughts still on the board. Using the numbers we found in the equations above, we could write:

$$7 - 5 = 2$$

You could also find how many more draughts Red has left than Black by comparing the number of draughts that have been taken. If you wrote that equation, it would look like this:

$$7 - 5 = 2$$

This equation also answers the last subtraction question, 'How many more draughts does Black have to take in order to have taken the same number as Red?'

8/9 The Gremlin's Gold
No answers.

10 It's Nothing, Really!
You should end up with seven rows that look like this:

17	12	5	15
5	7	10	2
2	3	8	3
1	5	5	1
4	0	4	0
4	4	4	4
0	0	0	0

You will always end up with a row of fours followed by a row of noughts.

11 Pasta Puzzle
The first pasta shapes stand for the numbers 24 and 32.
The problems are as follows:

25	40	and	32
-16	-32		-26
9	8		6

12/13 The Tortoise, the Hare and...
1. The cheetah, 70 miles per hour (mph)
2. The lion, 50 mph
3. The fox, 43 mph
4. The rabbit, 35 mph
5. The giraffe, 32 mph

6. The cat, 30 mph
7. The human, almost 28 mph
8. The pig, 11 mph
9. The chicken, 9 mph
10. The giant tortoise, less than 1 mph

14/15 Red Alert

According to the tally, 17 people wore red and 33 people did not; the 'No Red' group is larger. To find out how much larger, subtract 17 from 33; the difference is 16.

What were the results of your own tally? Do you think your results might have been different if you had chosen a different place to watch and tally? What about a soccer game? A dentist's waiting room?

If you tallied with a friend, did you ever see someone who was wearing both your favourite colour and your friend's? What did you do? Why?

16/17 Tower Challenge

Use subtraction to see how much more or less than 1.5 metres your total lengths are, and to determine how much closer to 1.5 metres one player is than another.

18/19 Shopping Spree

Correct combinations include:
1. £17 jeans, £46 jacket, £24 shoes and £63 skis
2. £17 jeans, £39 jacket, £24 shoes and £70 skis
3. £14 jeans, £46 jacket, £24 shoes and £66 skis
4. £14 jeans, £44 jacket, £29 shoes and £63 skis
5. £19 jeans, £44 jacket, £24 shoes and £63 skis
6. £19 jeans, £39 jacket, £29 shoes and £63 skis
7. £21 jeans, £39 jacket, £24 shoes and £66 skis

20 Pocket Money

Imran's money

Kelly's money

James's money

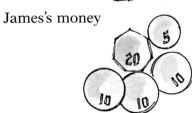

Rachel's money

29

Answers

21 Gallons of Guppies

It takes 32 days to give away all the guppies. The pattern is not exact; on the 32nd day, you only have 4 guppies left to give away.

22/23 And the Answer is...

No answers.

24/25 Code Breaking

Dear Bill,

Quick! There is no time to lose. Put the map under loose log on the hill. If all goes well, Leslie will pick it up and sell it. I beg you to follow this plan, or else!

Good luck,

Bob

26 A-Maze-ing 10,000

Follow the arrows to one possible solution to the maze.

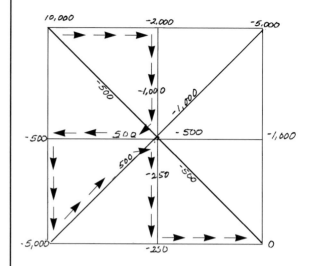

Glossary

consecutive Numbers that follow, one after another, in a sequence.

difference The amount by which a number is larger or smaller than another, or the amount left when you subtract one number from another.

digit A numeral from 0 to 9.

equation A mathematical sentence, or formula, that says two expressions are equal.

predict To try and guess the outcome of something.

subtraction The operation in which you find the difference between two numbers; the operation shown by the minus sign; the process in which you take away one number from another.

sum The quantity left when you add together two numbers.

tally To keep a count of something. Long ago, when two people wanted to keep an account, they made notches in a piece of wood called a tally. They split the tally into two matching halves, so that they each had one.

Index